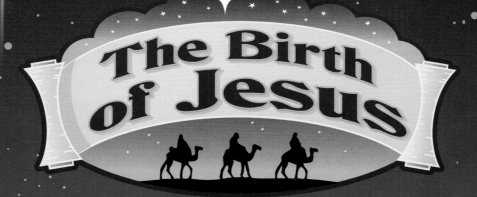

Illustrated by MADA Design, Inc.
Adapted and written by David Bauman

© 2005 by Meredith Corporation, Des Moines, Iowa.
First edition. All Rights Reserved.
Printed in Mexico
ISBN: 0-696-22827-0

Meredith® Books
Des Moines, Iowa

More than 2,000 years ago in Nazareth lived a young woman named Mary. Mary loved God and she was filled with goodness.

One night, the archangel Gabriel appeared and told Mary that she would have a baby who was the Son of God. Seeing an angel scared Mary, but Gabriel told her not to be afraid and he flew away.

Mary was not scared anymore, and she was happy that God chose her.

Mary was engaged to Joseph, a carpenter. When Mary told Joseph about Gabriel's visit, Joseph was confused. He left his carpenter's tools to walk and think. He soon rested and fell asleep.

In a dream, an angel appeared and told Joseph that Mary's child would be the savior of mankind. When the angel flew away, Joseph woke up and knew his dream came from God.

Joseph and Mary had their wedding.

Around this time, the ruler of the land said that all people must return to their hometowns to be counted.

Joseph and Mary headed home to Bethlehem. Because Mary was going to have a baby, she rode a donkey for the long trip. They traveled through towns and countryside where shepherds tended their flocks.

Joseph and Mary needed to find a place to stay in Bethlehem.

At the first inn, Joseph knocked on the door. The innkeeper yelled, "No room!" and slammed the door.

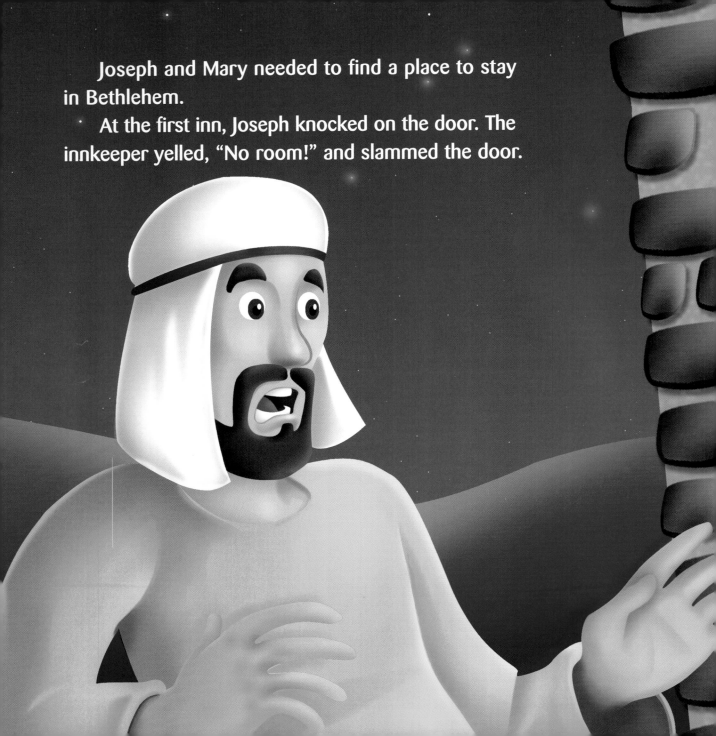

Joseph went from inn to inn. He knocked at each door. But every innkeeper slammed the door. Joseph worried that Mary would soon have the baby, so he moved on, with Mary riding the donkey.

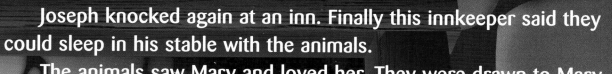

Joseph knocked again at an inn. Finally this innkeeper said they could sleep in his stable with the animals.

The animals saw Mary and loved her. They were drawn to Mary by her goodness. A dove flew down from the rafters, and the horses neighed. Joseph made a bed of hay for Mary so she could rest and wait for the baby to come.

The Son of God was born that night and they named him Jesus. Angels appeared. The animals called out their own greetings to the baby: doves cooed, horses neighed, and the donkeys brayed. Mary held the baby Jesus, and the music of her voice soothed the infant and all the animals. Mary and Joseph said prayers of thanks to God for the newborn son.

God put a very special, bright star in the sky when Jesus was born. The angels appeared to shepherds and brought the wonderful news. Many shepherds were scared. The angels told them to rejoice and not to be afraid.

With their flocks, the shepherds followed the star to Bethlehem. When the shepherds entered the stable, they heard the infant. They knelt quietly to pray.

The shepherds were not the only ones who saw the star.
Three men from the East, Wise Men who studied scriptures,
also saw the star and knew it would lead them west, to the newborn
Son of God who would be King of the Jews.
They packed their camels to prepare for the journey. They
brought with them special gifts for baby Jesus.

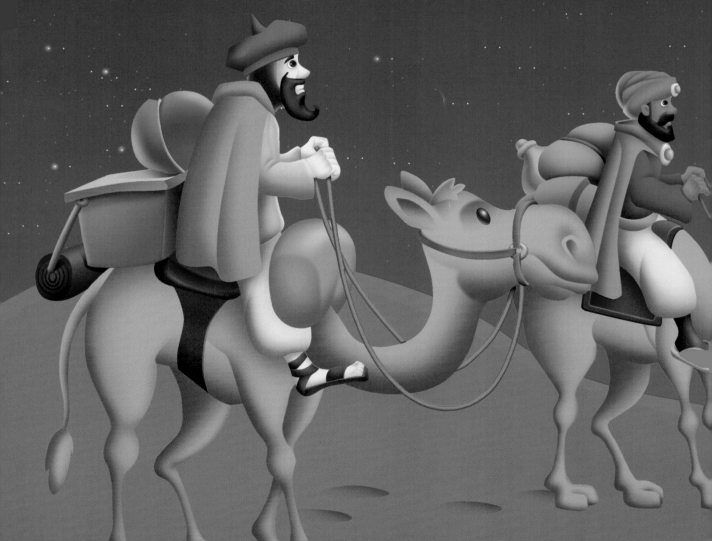

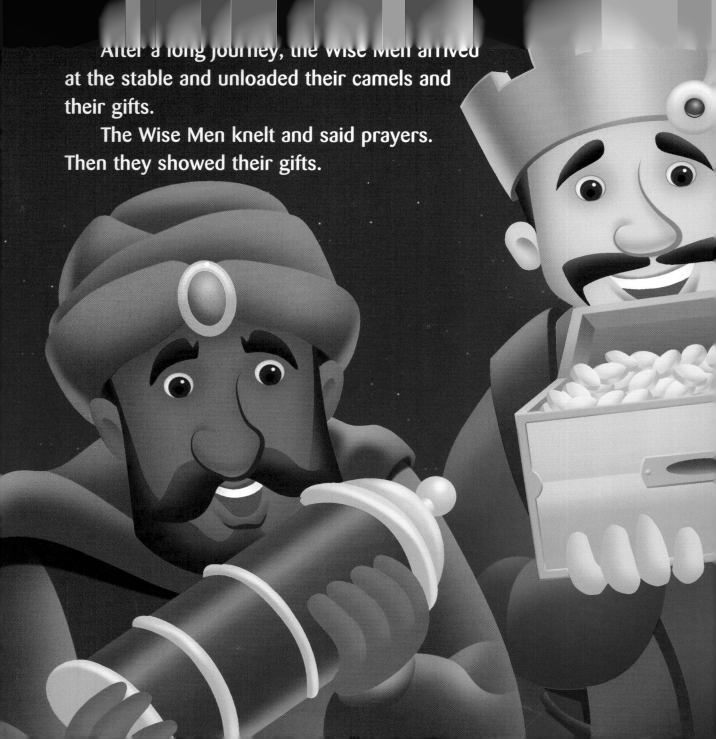

After a long journey, the Wise Men arrived at the stable and unloaded their camels and their gifts.

The Wise Men knelt and said prayers. Then they showed their gifts.

The first Wise Man brought a chest filled with gold. The second Wise Man brought a chest that held sweet-smelling incense. The third Wise Man's gift was bottles of myrrh, a rare perfume.

Joseph and Mary were amazed.

The stable was crowded with shepherds and Wise Men, animals and angels. It was filled with the music of Mary's voice and the sounds of sheep, horses, and doves.

Then the stable fell silent and all watched as Mary rocked the baby Jesus in her arms and quieted him with the music of her voice and prayers to God.